Jeremy Taylor

Story illustrated by
Steve May

Find out about

- Jobs – some are fantastic, some are boring and some are dangerous!

Tricky words

- fantastic
- chocolate
- really
- boring
- envelopes
- dangerous

Introduce these tricky words and help the reader when they come across them later!

Text starter

Some people say they have fantastic jobs and other people say their jobs are boring. Would you like to be a chocolate taster?

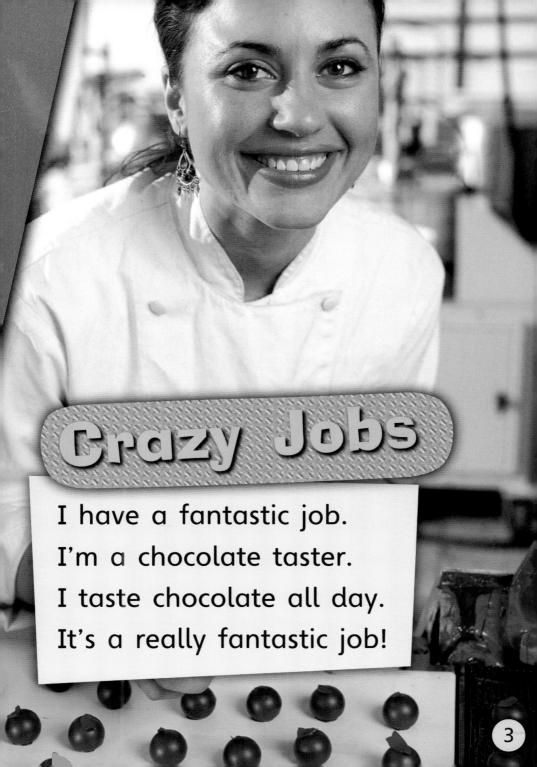

Crazy Jobs

I have a fantastic job.
I'm a chocolate taster.
I taste chocolate all day.
It's a really fantastic job!

I have a boring job. I put letters in envelopes all day. It's a really boring job.

I have a boring job.
I check carrots all day.

Carrots, carrots and more carrots all day. It's a really boring job.

I have a funny job.
I draw cartoons all day.
It's a very funny job.

I have a funny job.
I'm a clown. I work in a circus.
It's a very funny job.

I have a job on TV.
It's a fantastic job –
MOST of the time!

I have a dangerous job.
I look after crocodiles all day.
It's a really dangerous job.

I have a very dangerous job.
I'm a referee.
But it's a fantastic job –
MOST of the time!

Quiz

Text Detective

- What was the most dangerous job?
- What job would you like to do?

Word Detective

- Phonic Focus: Blending three phonemes

  Page 3: Can you sound out 'job'?
- Page 10: Which two words make up the word 'it's'?
- Page 10: Why is the word 'MOST' in capital letters?

Super Speller

Read these words:

have   very   more

Now try to spell them!

HA! HA! HA!

Q How does a farmer count his cows?

A With a cowculator.

In this story

 Tom

 Kim

Mum

 Uncle

 Grandad

Tricky words

- expensive
- money
- worked
- enough
- rollerblades

Introduce these tricky words and help the reader when they come across them later!

Story starter

Tom loves all kinds of sport. One day, he saw a bike in a shop window. But the bike was very expensive so Tom had to work to get some money.

I Want a New Bike!

"I want that bike," said Tom.
"That bike is so cool."

"That bike is very expensive," said Kim. "You will have to work to get some money."

So Tom worked. He worked very hard for his mum.

His mum gave him some money for his bike.

"Here you are, Tom," said Mum.

Tom worked very hard for his uncle.

Do you think Tom will get enough money to buy the bike?

His uncle gave him some money for his bike.

"Here you are, Tom," he said.

17

Tom worked very hard for his grandad.

His grandad gave him some money for his bike.

"Here you are, Tom," he said.

Tom had lots of money ...

"I have not got enough money for that bike," said Tom, "but I have got enough money for some rollerblades."

So Tom got some rollerblades.
"Cool," said Kim.

Quiz

- Did Tom get enough money to buy the bike?
- Have you ever saved up for something special?

Word Detective

- Phonic Focus: Blending three phonemes
  Page 15: Sound out the word 'him'.
- Page 22: Find two words which rhyme.
- Page 23: Why are there speech marks around
  the word 'cool'?

Super Speller

Read these words:

hard   for   gave

Now try to spell them!

HA! HA! HA!

Q Where can you buy a cheap boat?

A In a sail.